*A
gift
honoring
Griffin
and
Carson
Gilchrist*

The Sioux

A Proud People

R. Conrad Stein

Enslow Elementary
an imprint of
Enslow Publishers, Inc.
40 Industrial Road   PO Box 38
Box 398   Aldershot
Berkeley Heights, NJ 07922 Hants GU12 6BP
USA   UK
http://www.enslow.com

Editor's Note: The Lakota, Nakota, and Dakota people are often collectively referred to as the Sioux. We, at Enslow Publishers, Inc., are aware that "Sioux" is sometimes considered an offensive term. However, since this group of people are still primarily known as the Sioux, we have decided to use this term. We mean no disrespect to the Lakota, Nakota, or Dakota people, but just wish to reach as many readers as possible in order to tell the rich history and current accomplishments of this vibrant people

Enslow Elementary, an imprint of Enslow Publishers, Inc.

Enslow Elementary® is a registered trademark of Enslow Publishers, Inc.

Library of Congress Cataloging-in-Publication Data:

Stein, R. Conrad.
    The Sioux : a proud people / R. Conrad Stein.
       p. cm. — (American Indians)
    Includes bibliographical references and index.
    ISBN 0-7660-2452-0
    1. Dakota Indians—History—Juvenile literature. 2. Dakota Indians—Social life and customs—Juvenile literature. I. Title. II. Series. III. American Indians (Berkeley Heights, N.J.)
E99.D1S74 2005
978.004'975243--dc22

2004016146

To Our Readers: We have done our best to make sure all Internet addresses in this book were active and appropriate when we went to press. However, the author and the publisher have no control over and assume no liability for the material available on those Internet sites or on other Web sites they may link to. Any comments or suggestions can be sent by e-mail to comments@enslow.com or to the address on the back cover.

Illustration Credits: Associated Press, AP, pp. 1 (center), 9, 36, 37, 42, 43; © Bassouls Sophie/Corbis Sygma, p. 39 (bottom); Clipart.com, pp. 16, 18, 41; © Corel Corporation, pp. 7, 22, 27 (bottom); Enslow Publishers, Inc., p. 8; Getty Images, pp. 1 (right background), 31; © Marilyn "Angel" Wynn, Nativestock.com, pp. 1 (left), 4, 10, 15, 21, 30; Minnesota Historical Society, p. 38; Minnesota Historical Society, Gift of Otto L. Schmidt, p. 5; Photos.com, pp. 1 (right), 11, 17, 26, 32, 44; Nativestock Pictures, Nativestock.com, p. 23; Photo courtesy of the U.S. Army, p. 29; Reproduced from the Collections of the Library of Congress, pp. 1 (left background), 14, 19, 24, 25, 28, 34, 39 (top); Reproduced from *Ready-To-Use Old West Cuts: 183 Different Copyright-Free Designs Printed One Side*, published by Dover Publications, Inc., in 1995, p. 27 (top); Sun Valley Photography, Nativestock.com, p. 6; Time Life Pictures/Getty Images, p. 33; Western History Collection, Denver Public Library, pp. 20, 35.

Cover Illustration: Associated Press, AP, (center); Getty Images, (right background); © Marilyn "Angel" Wynn, Nativestock.com, (left); Photos.com, (right); Reproduced from the Collections of the Library of Congress (left background).

Contents

This Sioux boy dances at a pow-wow on Pine Ridge Reservation in South Dakota.

❖ Sioux Pride ❖

"I will remain what I am until I die, a hunter . . ."

These words were spoken by Sitting Bull, a leader of the Lakota people. In Sitting Bull's youth, the Lakota lived on the Great Plains. The Lakota, along with the Nakota and Dakota, make up a group of people often called the Sioux. They were and are a mighty nation. Today the Sioux still live on the Great Plains. They operate businesses and work to maintain their traditions. Only by looking into the Sioux's past, can we begin to understand how they celebrate their traditions today.

This is an 1857 painting of a Sioux camp on the Mississippi River.

chapter one

The Land

The Great Plains is a huge, mostly flat region that lies in the middle of the United States. The Sioux include the Lakota, Nakota, and Dakota people. The Sioux live in the northern Great Plains. Many Sioux reside in North and South Dakota.

The Sioux Then

Long ago the Great Plains was a sea of grass. In late summer, the grasses grew as high as a horse's neck. Vast herds of buffalo, or bison, roamed the region. The Sioux hunted buffalo in many ways. Sometimes they put buffalo hides over their backs. Then they sneaked up on the herds. When close, they shot arrows at

During the winter months, the Sioux sometimes used snowshoes to hunt buffalo.

the animals. Europeans brought
horses to the Great Plains in the
1600s and 1700s. When Sioux hunters acquired horses,
they chased the buffalo on horseback.

Horses helped the Sioux become even greater hunters.

Rising out of the Great Plains is an area called the
Black Hills. The Black Hills was the religious center of
the Sioux nation. Tribal priests told a legend that said the
Sioux once lived in a paradise beneath the Black Hills.
But they were not satisfied in paradise. The people longed

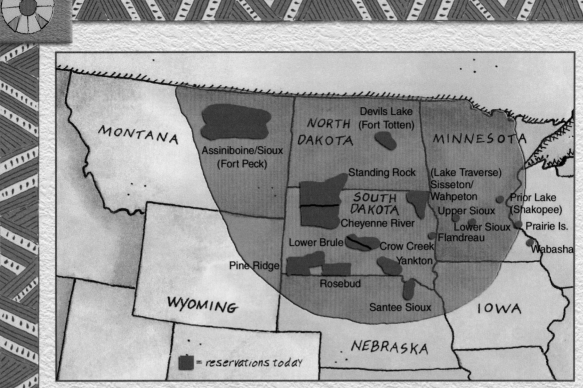

The pink area shows the land the Sioux once called their home. The blue areas are the reservations where many Sioux live today.

to see the outside. A tribal elder warned them that the outside world was filled with troubles. The people did not listen. They left through a mountain opening called Wind Cave. Once outside, they were never again able to return to paradise.

The Sioux Today

The majority of Sioux people remain in the northern Great Plains. More than thirty thousand Dakota live on reservations in North Dakota alone. The Sioux are not required to live on reservations. They are free to come and go as they please. Sioux men and women hold jobs in large cities.

Many Sioux prefer to live on reservations because they have family members and close friends there. In recent years, thriving businesses have developed on reservation land. The Sioux Manufacturing Corporation on the Spirit Lake Nation Reservation makes equipment for the United States government. Plastic bags are made at Dakota Western, a factory on the Lake Traverse Reservation. These factories are owned and managed largely by Sioux people.

Burton "Joe" Jackson holds a piece of Kevlar made at the Sioux Manufacturing Corporation. Kevlar is used to make armor for American soldiers.

chapter two

History

In the 1600s, the Sioux lived in the forests of what is now Minnesota. French explorers visited the region. The French asked a nearby group of people, the Chippewa, about the people who lived in the tall woodlands. The Chippewa called the woodland people the Sioux, which meant "little snakes." The Chippewa were bitter enemies of the Sioux and gave them that name. The Sioux people called themselves the Dakota, Lakota, or Nakota. In their language, the word "Lakota" meant "friend."

American Indian wars caused the Sioux to move from the forest. Some spread out along the Missouri River. The river itself was named after a Sioux group called the Missouri,

This buffalo bone tool even had its own carrying case.

or "wooden canoe people." The vast majority of Sioux settled in what is now North

The Sioux would often dance before a battle. They believed that this would help them win.

and South Dakota, Nebraska, Wyoming, and Montana. There, in the grasslands, the buffalo provided everything the people needed. They ate the animal's meat. They used buffalo hides as coats. They fashioned buffalo bones into tools, toys for children, and musical instruments.

In 1876, white miners sought gold in the Black Hills. The Sioux believed the Black Hills were the final resting grounds for their dead. An angry Sioux nation went to war. In June 1876, the Lakota, Cheyenne, and Arapaho defeated a unit of the U.S. 7th Cavalry Regiment at the Battle of the Little Bighorn. The unit was led by a famous colonel named George A. Custer. It was the worst defeat the cavalry ever suffered during its long history of warfare with American Indians. The battle was later called "Custer's Last Stand" by the Americans.

The victory at the Little Bighorn brought no peace for the Lakota or the rest of the Sioux. By the late 1870s, all Sioux people were forced onto reservations. In December 1890, almost three hundred Lakota Sioux were

1874: Gold is discovered in the Black Hills. Hundreds of gold seekers come to the area.

Before the 1600s: People speaking Sioux-type languages settle in what is now Minnesota. They then spread north to Canada.

1868: The U.S. gives the Black Hills to the Sioux.

1877: The Black Hills becomes the property of the U.S.

1600   1700   1800   1850   1860   1870

Most Sioux moved to the Great Plains region.

1876: George Custer's men are defeated by Lakota Sioux, Cheyenne, and Arapaho at the Battle of the Little Bighorn in present-day Montana.

killed by the United States Army at Wounded Knee, South Dakota. Many of those killed were women, children, and old men. Wounded Knee was the last large-scale clash between the army and American Indians. Today many historians claim that Wounded Knee was not really a battle at all. Instead, Wounded Knee was a massacre, committed on purpose by the United States Army against the Lakota people.

Sioux pride was never defeated. Family groups remained close. Parents encouraged their children to do well in school. Strong families allowed the people to enter the modern world with confidence.

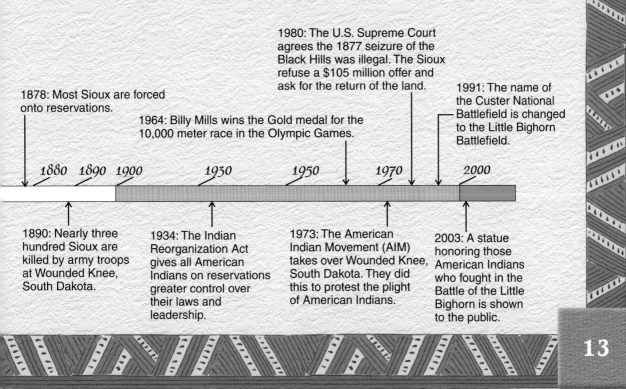

1980: The U.S. Supreme Court agrees the 1877 seizure of the Black Hills was illegal. The Sioux refuse a $105 million offer and ask for the return of the land.

1878: Most Sioux are forced onto reservations.

1964: Billy Mills wins the Gold medal for the 10,000 meter race in the Olympic Games.

1991: The name of the Custer National Battlefield is changed to the Little Bighorn Battlefield.

1880 1890 1900   1930   1950   1970   2000

1890: Nearly three hundred Sioux are killed by army troops at Wounded Knee, South Dakota.

1934: The Indian Reorganization Act gives all American Indians on reservations greater control over their laws and leadership.

1973: The American Indian Movement (AIM) takes over Wounded Knee, South Dakota. They did this to protest the plight of American Indians.

2003: A statue honoring those American Indians who fought in the Battle of the Little Bighorn is shown to the public.

chapter three

Homes

When the Sioux were a hunting people, they followed herds of buffalo across the Great Plains. Because they were always on the move, they lived in a dwelling called the tipi. Today, they look for a safe home.

The Sioux Then

A tipi was a portable house. Tipis were cone shaped. They were put together by women. The women tied together long poles at the top of the cone. They then spread the poles out to form a broad circle at the bottom. The women covered the poles with buffalo hides.

Tipis could be put up or taken down in less than an hour. Horses and dogs helped move the poles

The first step of building a tipi was to tie together wooden poles to make the frame.

and the hides from place to place. Often a rattle was tied over the entrance. The rattle served as a "doorbell" for anyone wanting to come inside. Men painted pictures on the tipi's outside. But it was understood the tipis were owned by women. A man had to get his wife's permission before he began decorating the tipi with pictures.

The Sioux Today

Today, Sioux on reservations live in modern houses made of brick or wood. Some families live in small trailers. Other families have cabins without electric lights. Some Sioux still use tipis for ceremonies.

This modern tipi has feathers painted on it.

chapter four

Clothing

Buffalo and other wild animals provided the Sioux with their clothes as well as their food. Today, the Sioux reserve special dress for certain celebrations.

The Sioux Then

Women and little girls wore dresses made from deerskin, or sometimes buffalo hide. Boys and men wore buffalo-hide leggings. Buffalo-hide coats kept everyone warm in the winter months.

Sioux women made deerskin clothes and moccasins for the family. Clothes for a special occasion, such as a marriage dress, were often a work of art. Women inserted

A Sioux family works on animal skins and does beadwork.

brightly colored porcupine quills into deerskin pants or a dress. The quills were arranged in beautiful designs. Elk teeth and shells were also sewn onto an article of clothing. Days and days of work were devoted to a marriage dress. When European and American settlers arrived, the Sioux traded for glass beads that they sewed onto clothes.

The Sioux Today

Modern Sioux buy clothes at a store like everyone else. But schools on reservations are reviving the old Sioux art of making clothes. Children are taught how to make moccasins and shirts from leather. Contests are held and awards are given for the best designs.

A Sioux headdress can be very colorful.

chapter five

Food and Meals

The Sioux were skilled hunters. Animals of the Great Plains provided for most of their needs. Traditional recipes are still made today.

The Sioux Then

Buffalo meat was the favorite dish of the Sioux people. The buffalo hump was the tastiest. Shoulders contained a lot of meat, and they were eaten on feast days. For everyday meals, women made a stew of buffalo meat mixed with roots and berries. The Sioux also ate fish, wild turkey, deer, and elk. Because they followed the roaming buffalo, the people did little farming. But the Sioux were experts in gathering wild foods such as Juneberries, turnips, and onions.

Sioux men and boys worked together to hunt buffalo.

Two Dakota Sioux cut and hang meat to dry in 1908.
Dried meat did not spoil as quickly as raw meat.

The Sioux Today

The modern Sioux diet is much the same as that of most other Americans. Modern eating habits have reduced the people's once excellent health. White bread and sweet snacks have made many Sioux, along with many Americans, overweight. The disease diabetes was unknown to the Sioux before 1940. Many thousands of Sioux adults now have diabetes. The Sioux are studying the science of nutrition as a way of helping people with the disease.

chapter six

Family Life

Loving families have always been the Sioux people's greatest strength and source of support.

The Sioux Then

A young man sings outside the tipi of a girl he likes. The girl's family invites him inside. If the girl does not like the young man, she will turn her back on him. If she likes him, she will smile. Her smile means she will probably get married. When a girl reached the age for courtship, she painted the right side of her face red. She also wore a feather in her hair. Most girls were married between the ages of twelve and fifteen.

Sioux parents allowed small children to play and

A Dakota Sioux girl pulls another child in a wagon in 1898. The girl's dress is decorated with shells.

explore their world. Rarely did they scold or spank a child. Children knew it was important to be good to other family members.

The Sioux Today

Today young Sioux men and women go on dates before they decide to get married. Modern Sioux still tend to have close families.

However, some Sioux suffer from alcoholism. Abuse of alcohol leads to family violence. The Sioux now promote family safety. One group called TEAM (Tribal Empowerment Anti Drug/Violence Movement) educates people about the dangers of alcohol and other drugs. Despite having problems that many American families have, most Sioux live proud, happy lives.

Steven Garcia and his daughter Cheyenne live on the Pine Ridge Reservation in South Dakota.

chapter seven

Everyday Life

Work and fun fill the lives of Sioux people. This is as true today as it was ages ago.

The Sioux Then

Life for the Sioux and other Plains Indians changed with the seasons. The summers were very hot on the Great Plains. During the winter months, families huddled inside their tipis while blizzards piled up snow outside. People told their age by how many winters they had survived.

During the summer, the Sioux hunted and kept an eye out for intruders. This group of riders spots a wagon train of settlers in the distance.

A Brule Sioux Medicine man works on a winter count, which he is painting on deer hide.

A twelve year old would say: "I have seen twelve winters." Tribal historians kept written records through what was called a "winter count." Pictures on the winter count told how the tribe endured during the cold months. A picture of several bodies laid out in a line meant there were many deaths due to sickness in that particular year.

The Sioux Today

Daily life now depends on whether one lives on a reservation or in the cities. Sioux people in the cities hurry to jobs or to school as do their neighbors. The pace of life on a reservation is slower, but the work is sometimes harder. Most reservation Sioux are up before the sun rises. Many are farmers. Like farmers everywhere, they have dozens of chores to perform.

chapter eight

Religion and Medicine

"Be kind to all men and animals—do nothing to harm your family or the families of others"—Instructions given in a dream to the Sioux spiritual leader Black Horse.

The Sioux Then

To the Sioux, the natural world and the spiritual world were one and the same. All life was a gift from the creator spirit *Wakan Tanka*. The words "Wakan Tanka" are translated as "all that is holy and mysterious."

The Sioux believed lesser spirits called *Wakanpi* ruled specific things such as

This medicine man, named Fool Bull, had his picture taken in 1900.

sickness and health. Tribal doctors prayed to these lesser spirits before attempting to heal the sick. A common Sioux treatment was the "sweat lodge." A sick person went into a small hut heated by a fire. Once inside the lodge, he or she "sweated out" sicknesses such as fever or headaches. A sweat-lodge session was also a religious experience as it brought a person closer to the spirits.

Certain Great Plains plants were also used as medicine. Wild licorice eased the pain of a toothache.

The fire was positioned in the center of a sweat lodge frame. Then, the frame was covered with animal hides.

Some Sioux now worship at their local church, like this one in Rockville, Utah.

The Sioux Today

The old religion faded when the Sioux were forced onto reservations during the late 1800s. People called missionaries got most of the Sioux to become Christians.

Many modern Sioux believe in a legend that says the White Buffalo Calf Woman will bring the buffalo back to the Great Plains. In 1990, the Sioux and other Plains

Indians formed the Intertribal Bison Cooperative, with a membership of forty-two tribes. The group tends to a herd of about eight thousand buffalo. The Plains people hope their spiritual lives and their health will thrive when buffalo once more roam the grasslands.

Trains and hunters were two of the causes that led to the loss of many buffalo. Today, the Sioux are working to increase the numbers of the American buffalo.

chapter nine

Arts and Music

"One of the best ways to understand a people is to know what makes them laugh." —The modern Sioux writer Vine Deloria, Jr.

The Sioux Then

A pipe carved from stone was the prized object of most Sioux. The pipe was often a piece of art. Religious symbols were painted on the pipe's stem. Its tobacco bowl was sculpted into marvelous human figures.

The Sioux worked the hardest at the art of dance. Men and women danced for hours or even days without stopping. The Sioux felt the tiring dances allowed a person to see the spirit world. This was like catching a glimpse of heaven. Some dances were painful. In the Sun Dance,

This Dakota Sioux holds a long pipe in 1907.

young men pierced their skin with porcupine quills or pieces of wood. Other dances were fun. During the Crazy Dance, people were required to sing or chant backward.

The Sioux Today

Dancing is the featured activity at modern-day events called pow-wows. Pow-wows allow people of several groups to get together, discuss their problems, share their joys, and dance. Many Sioux artists today make crafts such as dolls, necklaces, and bracelets. These marvelous craft pieces are sold on Sioux reservations and in art galleries.

Jeff Bailey, a Lakota Sioux and member of the Black Bear Singers/Dancers, dances at the Pentagon. The Pentagon is a building where American military leaders work.

chapter ten

Sports and Games

"Some boys got hurt, but afterward we would talk and laugh about it. Very seldom did any fellow get mad." —A Sioux man named Iron Shell, describing a team sport similar to soccer.

The Sioux Then

A popular boys' game was played with a hoop made from tree branches. One boy rolled the hoop over the grass. Another boy tried to throw a small spear through the center of the rolling hoop without knocking it down. In this way, a boy learned to hunt rabbits and squirrels.

Girls enjoyed playing a blanket-toss game. Five or six girls pulled on a buffalo-hide blanket. The smallest girl in the group lay in the

This model shows two boys playing the hoop-and-spear game.

This Sioux family goes sledding in January 1926.

center of the blanket and bounced with the tugs. Boys and girls both sledded in the winter. Sleds were often made from the curved bones of a buffalo. Contests were held to see who could slide the farthest.

The favorite team sport among the Sioux was a soccer game called *shinny*. The soccer ball was made from animal skins. The goals were two tipis at opposite ends of the camp. Each team tried to kick the ball into the opposing tipi. There were no boundaries. One team tried to exhaust another team by running far. Girls played a form of shinny with sticks.

The Sioux Today

Modern Sioux enjoy all popular team sports—baseball, football, basketball, and soccer. Teams from different reservations play each other. A basketball tournament called the Lakota Nation Invitational (LNI) is held once a year in Rapid City, South Dakota. High school teams participate in the LNI as hundreds of fans cheer. Girls' field hockey is a popular team sport played in reservation schools. Today's field hockey is similar to the girls' shinny of the past.

The Sioux enjoy playing basketball.

The star runner and Marine lieutenant Billy Mills was born on Pine Ridge Reservation in South Dakota in 1938. In 1964 he went to the Olympic Games in Tokyo, Japan, to run the 10,000-meter race. Experts gave him no chance to win. No American had ever won the 10,000-meter event. But Mills surprised the experts. He captured first place and won the gold medal. Billy Mills became a hero in the United States. His story was told in the 1983 movie *Running Brave.*

Billy Mills (left) is on his way to winning the Gold Medal in this picture!

chapter eleven

Warfare

For the most part, the Sioux lived in peace with their neighbors. However, when forced to wage war, they were fierce fighters. Today, they once again live in peace.

The Sioux Then

In battle, Sioux warriors were fearless. A common Sioux battle cry was "It is a good day to die." The Sioux's most famous battle was fought by the Lakota in 1876 at the Little Bighorn River in present-day Montana. Leading the Lakota into battle were two chiefs: Sitting Bull and Crazy Horse.

Sitting Bull poses for a picture, holding his peace pipe.

Sitting Bull (1851–1890) was the religious leader of the Lakota people. Before the battle, he performed the painful Sun Dance. After dancing for hours without food or sleep, he fell into a trance. While unconscious, he had a powerful vision. He saw white soldiers falling upside down into the Lakota camp. Sitting Bull predicted victory in the coming battle.

Crazy Horse (1849–1877) led Lakota horsemen into

The Battle of the Little Bighorn was a clear victory for Crazy Horse's men.

battle. He was famous for surprising his enemies with lightning-quick attacks. In June 1876, Crazy Horse surprised Lieutenant Colonel George Custer by launching a bold attack. All 250 soldiers under Custer's immediate command were killed.

The Sioux Today

The Sioux still fight for their rights. However, their fight is now largely confined to the courtroom. The Black Hills

Holy Rock, an Oglala Sioux government official, stands in the Black Hills region. Prayer cloths hang from the tree behind him. People hung them there because the Black Hills is sacred ground to the Sioux.

Most of these marchers are members of the Cheyenne River Sioux tribe. They follow a wagon carrying the body of Private Sheldon Hawk Eagle. He was killed in Iraq in 2003.

region remains sacred to the Sioux soul. In 1876, the United States government took over the Black Hills. The Sioux have sued in court claiming the takeover was illegal. In 1980, the U.S. Supreme Court agreed the land was wrongfully taken from the tribe. The court awarded the Sioux people $105 million for land. They refused to take the money. Instead, their lawyers demanded the Black Hills be returned. To this day, the Black Hills case is pending in the courts.

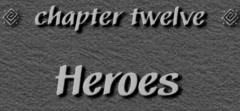
Heroes

"Come on and soar, we are eagles!" —This quote comes from an old Sioux legend about two eagles mistakenly put in a coop with chickens.

The Sioux Past

Crazy Horse and Sitting Bull will always be heroes of the Lakota, a Sioux group. Black Elk (1863–1950) and Dr. Charles Eastman (1858–1939) are also important to Sioux history. Black Elk was a storyteller who preserved many Sioux tales in the book *Black Elk Speaks*. Eastman was a Dakota and founded both the Boy Scouts of America and the Camp Fire Girls.

Black Elk was a great storyteller.

The Sioux Today

Vine Deloria Jr. (born 1933) is a modern Sioux hero. He writes books on the American Indian experience. One of his books is called *Custer Died for Your Sins.*

Mary Crow Dog (born 1953) is a writer and activist. An activist is a person who works for a cause. She grew up on the Rosebud Sioux Reservation in South Dakota. She lived in a one-room log cabin that had no electricity or plumbing. At a young age, she joined the organization called American Indian Movement (AIM). In 1990 she published *Lakota Women.* She continues to write and work for American Indian causes.

Dr. Charles Eastman wore a headdress for this 1931 photo (top). Mary Crow Dog (bottom) is a modern-day inspiring Sioux writer.

chapter thirteen

Government

"Go to your leader and tell him to have a council tipi set up in the center of the village." —A message from the White Buffalo Calf Woman, as told in an old Sioux story.

The Sioux Then

Long before white settlers came to the Great Plains, the Sioux people divided into three major groups. The Dakota lived in what is now Minnesota, the Nakota in North and South Dakota, and the Lakota in the western Dakotas and in Nebraska. Each of the three groups practiced their own form of government. Decision making was done at meetings held by respected men.

Most groups had several chiefs. Any older man could become a chief. The views of women were respected. But a woman could not lead a tribe or a village. Many chiefs were war heroes who had grown too old to fight. Above

The chief was a respected leader of the Sioux and has many feathers in his headdress.

all, the Sioux chiefs were expected to rule with great wisdom.

Male societies also had a part in Sioux government meetings. These societies could be thought of as men's clubs. One society was called the *Ska Yuhas*, meaning the White Horse Owners. These men did not necessarily own white horses. The *Ska Yuhas* were considered the tribe's best hunters. Older men joined a society called the *Naca Ominicias*. The older men were respected for their wisdom. However, the name *Naca Ominicias* translates into "Big Bellies."

The Sioux Today

The year 2000 census put the Sioux population at 108,272. This ranks the Sioux as the third largest

American Indian group in the United States. According to the 2000 census, the top four groups are:

Cherokee	*281,069*
Navaho	*269,202*
Sioux	*108,272*
Chippewa	*105,908*

Sioux Tribal Chairman Charlie Murphy (right) meets with United States officials on a construction project. Murphy is a leader of the Standing Rock Reservation.

Women are now just as active as men in the Sioux government. Teresa Peterson is vice chairwoman of the Upper Sioux.

Modern Sioux living on reservations hold regular elections. The people choose candidates for offices such as chairman or treasurer. No longer are women excluded from Sioux government. Anyone over the age of eighteen can vote in the elections. Women often run for offices in reservation government.

A Mighty People

In the distant past, the Sioux ruled the Great Plains. They were a hunting society. They lived in harmony with nature. Then white civilization spread to the Great Plains. The Sioux endured a painful period of warfare. Finally, most of them started a new life on reservations.

Today the Sioux face a number of challenges. Jobs are limited on the reservations. Young people often drop out of high school. But the Sioux are working every day to overcome these problems. Leaders urge the young to study Sioux history and learn of the days when their ancestors were the mightiest people on the Great Plains. The leaders also point to the future with hope. Always, Sioux pride will uplift the people's spirit.

A Sioux boy from South Dakota smiles. He is wearing a headdress and sitting in front of a painted tipi.

Words to Know

courtship—To try and win the favor or love of a person.

elder—An older, respected person.

harmony—To live in peace and cooperation with nature or other people.

nutrition—The study of eating habits.

pending—To be unsettled.

revive—To renew or bring up again.

shinny—A Sioux game that is a lot like soccer.

symbol—Something that represents something else.

trance—A sleeplike state.

Wakanpi—Spirits in which the Sioux believed.

More Books!

Bial, Raymond. *The Sioux*. Tarrytown, New York: Marshall Cavendish, 1999.

Eder Jeanne Oyawin. *Indian Nations: The Dakota Sioux*. New York: Raintree Steck-Vaughn Publishers, 2000.

Freedman, Russell. *The Life and Death of Crazy Horse*. New York: Holiday House, 1996.

Koestler-Grack, Rachel A. *The Sioux: Nomadic Buffalo Hunters*. Mankato, Minn.: Blue Earth Books, 2003.

McLeese, Don. *Sitting Bull*. Vero Beach, Fla.: Rourke Publishing, 2003.

Remington, Gwen. *Indigenous People of North America: The Sioux*. San Diego: Lucent Books, 2000.

Stein, R. Conrad. *The Battle of the Little Bighorn*. Danbury, Conn.: Children's Press, 1997.

Internet Addresses

Sioux Indians

<http://www.newadvent.org/cathen/14017a.htm>

Standing Rock Sioux Tribe

<http://www.standingrock.org>

Yankton Sioux Tribal Tourism Association

<http://yanktonsiouxtourism.com>

Index